ANNE MACDUFF
SAROUCHE RAZI
KIRSTEN HOFFMAN

Once upon a time in Australia:

Conversations about how our
MeToo movement exposed the
troubles with truth in law

First published 2024
Counterpress, Coventry
http://counterpress.org.uk

ISBN: 978-1-910761-19-9 (Paperback)

ISBN: 978-1-910761-20-5 (ePDF)

Sarouche and Anne, teachers at the law school I am at, whose dialogue I am about to present, say I am in exile from law school and might find my people overseas like Sarouche.

In 'Victoria' though, where I studied animation, I was told I would find my people in Canberra.

And in 'Western Australia', where I grew up, I was told I would find my people in 'Victoria'.

ANNE

When I was ten, I had a paper run. Every Wednesday afternoon, I would deliver a local newspaper to the houses in my suburb on my bike. It would take about three hours.

In the winter, it would sometimes be dark and cold before I had finished. When it got dark, and people arrived home and turned on their lights, I could sometimes see inside the houses. I would catch glimpses of their inside lives: what they did when they got home, how they decorated their houses, and a sense of the people who lived there. From the outside, I remember thinking how warm and cosy their homes looked.

Fast forward a decade or two, and I enrolled in a law degree at university. I seemed to notice things that other students didn't. I paid attention to the facts of cases that were not relevant, challenged the premise of a question when I should have been answering it, and saw issues of systemic injustice when I ought to have identified a substantive legal issue. Other law students did not seem to have this problem. How did they 'just know' what was the relevant, appropriate or pertinent thing to say or write? Why was my legal relevance relevant-meter so out of whack with everyone else's?

I felt ten years old again. I was a child on a cold night, peering into a bright, cosy home. From the outside, the law seemed familiar, inviting even. I could see inside, I could even go inside. But the house was arranged in a way that didn't seem to make natural sense to me. And despite the fact that I now work as a researcher in the law, doing law still doesn't come naturally. Rather, being a legal scholar is like a character-costume that I put on for special occasions.

Fast forward quite a few more decades, and in 2020 – 2021 I witnessed the airing of revelations of sexual harassment and assault in the legal profession, and in Parliament. Like many, I was appalled but not surprised. But then, when the Attorney-General, Christian Porter, attempted to use the concept of the rule of law to protect himself from accountability, I was angry. Why should he be able to unilaterally manipulate the legal furniture so that it best suited him? Why does he get to determine for himself what part of the picture is legally relevant? It seemed to me to be one of the most egregious displays of power and privilege that I had ever seen.

Damn it. If Mr Porter can bend the law to his shape and needs, why shouldn't I? Why shouldn't I talk about this issue in the way I would like? And what would it look like if I did? I am sure that at the very least, it would not be in my 'legal scholar' voice that pays attention to the legal-relevance meter.

I decided to sound out whether Sarouche might want to have a conversation with me about it...

SAROUCHE

For years I've been waiting for a silk to come and tap me on the shoulder and say, 'We're onto you. You're not one of us.' It's been sixteen years of practice, and I'm still waiting for it to happen.

I've always felt like an outsider to law. I felt like that in law school as people were getting into the rituals of moots, clerkships and legal precedent. I felt like that when I was working in Capital Markets, walking up Martin Place, and enjoying Sydney Harbour Bridge views. I felt like that as Principal of a community legal centre with my staff seeking support from me about why they should stick to their legal practice duties when the human response required breaking them.

I suppose I've always felt that I could see through the performativity of law. The rituals, the aesthetics and costumes, the tone of objectivity. I just can't quite drink the Kool-Aid, but I've been sure to hide my reservations in different ways: sometimes I perform the role like I were cast in play, sometimes I draw on authentic experiences into moments, and a lot of the time I feel angry about how much law is about the performance of power and how it's so inaccessible like that.

I was raised in other cultures, and English is my second language. I feel in Farsi. I believe in something much bigger than the material world. These things make my experience of law different. When I hear the Azan, it's so clear to me that I'm listening to law. And so the implicit claims of the Western Legal Tradition like its universality, its neutrality, and its sense of justice, well, it's not that they fall apart, but that they never really came together for me.

I see how the law treats victims of violence, and I see how the law treats offenders of violence – the law leaves both parties worse off in most cases that I've seen. When Anne made a callout to the ANU College of Law in response to the events that led to the March 4 Justice, I wanted to talk to her. Things can only be otherwise if we let them...

Now Anne and Sarouche begin their dialogue, and please forgive their writing for being stiff in the beginning. We kept this story true to the three of us growing in awareness and there will be sequels.

Hi Sarouche. It was an absolute delight to talk to you earlier today. ☺ We had a lot of momentum after the staff meeting and I'm a little disappointed nothing much has happened since then. I'm thinking about how we can do things differently, so I'm excited about starting this conversation with you.

ANNE

After it was revealed that the Attorney-General Christian Porter was at the centre of the historical rape allegations, the government initially refused to take any action. Supported by Prime Minister Morrison, Porter refused to step down from his role, claiming that to do so would be 'undermining the rule of law'.

Specifically, he declared that he should be treated as innocent until he was proved guilty by a court. What do you think are some of the assumptions behind this response and how do they impact on the public recognition of the harm of sexual assault?

18

One of the defining moments of last year for me was attending the March 4 Justice Rally in Canberra. There was an energy in the air – for a moment it felt like we were at a tipping point to entangle ourselves better in the struggle for gender justice. I remember a similar moment when I was living in Melbourne after Eurydice Dixon was killed. The air was thick with rage, but there was also hope in numbers. I'm very aware that there's a different kind of accountability for me as a cis-gendered male, and there is always a question here about whether I should be taking up space. I feel at the same time though, that we have a responsibility to be part of this conversation.

19

SAROUCHE

Grace Tame is also a comedic illustrator and has high-functioning autism.

I'm drawing an arc here to the events concerning Brittany Higgins, because I keep returning to the truth-making function we place on law. There's a Latin maxim that underpins legal process, 'Res iudicata pro veritate habetur'. It means 'an adjudicated thing is regarded as the truth'. I find the relationship between law and truth troubling, and within this the need for singularity within truth. Why can't we believe victims, while also allowing a legal process to play out?

It seems in part we're so steadfast in some idealised possibility of objectivity that a jury or judge can arrive at, as though they are not changed and influenced by their life experiences. Our colleague and scholar Hannah McGlade, on reflecting on the trial of Zachary Rolfe, is right to point to implicit structural racism when a jury has no Aboriginal people, in a jurisdiction that has about a 30% Aboriginal population.

Interestingly, for Brittany Higgins, Parliament finally has been able to hold the truth in complexity.* Following a recommendation from the Jenkins Review, the former Prime Minister made a formal apology to Brittany Higgins. The Rule of Law hasn't collapsed, despite this apology.

* Although see W.T.A.F. on page 72.

Many of our colleagues will staunchly defend the rules of procedural fairness as sacrosanct, and that they, more than anything, protect vulnerable people. And yet, it's Aboriginal and Torres Strait Islander men and women in prison in grossly disproportionate rates, and female victims of sexual violence continue to be traumatised and re-traumatised through their encounters with the criminal justice system. Do you see problems with how we conceptualise procedural fairness?

25

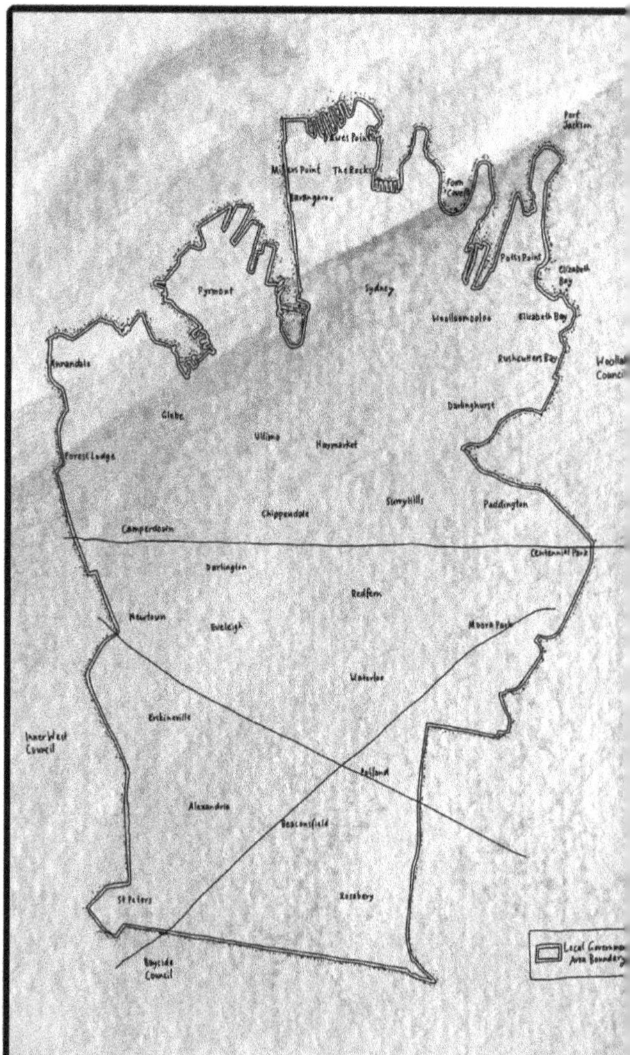
Port Jackson
The Rocks
Pyrmont
Sydney
Potts Point
Elizabeth Bay
Woolloomooloo
Elizabeth Bay
Rushcutters Bay
Annandale
Darlinghurst
Glebe
Ultimo
Haymarket
Forest Lodge
Surry Hills
Paddington
Chippendale
Camperdown
Centennial Park
Darlington
Redfern
Newtown
Eveleigh
Moore Park
Waterloo
Erskineville
Inner West Council
Alexandria
Beaconsfield
St Peters
Rosebery
Bayside Council

Hi Sarouche, I think you might have done your Doctoral Confirmation today? Amy mentioned something about it. If you did, have a great evening. If you haven't yet – good luck!

ANNE

But back to your question... absolutely. There are lots of problems with how we conceptualise procedural fairness. Of course, process is necessary and it provides some safeguards, but it is not sufficient to guarantee fairness. Procedures apply to a context, and the outcome is therefore context dependent.

Those who have privileged voices can conceptualise and apply procedures in ways that suit their interests. Sometimes that can be pushing procedures in particular (legitimate) ways. Sometimes it can mean using other resources (money, capacity) to draw a debate (or litigation) in particular ways. The outcome is indeed as you suggest. Aboriginal men and women are in prison at grossly disproportionate rates, and female victims of sexual violence continue to be traumatised and re-traumatised through their encounters with the criminal justice system.

If you will allow me a brief tangent, it reminds me of the debate between Hart and Fuller which is often raised in law schools. And while there are many valid criticisms against both theorists, there is a point that is relevant here. Basically Hart, a positivist, argues that a valid law is one that has passed through the processes that are stated to lead to a valid law. Fuller, on the other hand, argues that for a law to be valid, it must also comply with certain moral requirements. While I have some hesitations with Fuller's theory (I am not a natural law theorist), and the debate, it does underscore the point that what positivists recognise as 'law' does not guarantee a just outcome. This does align with my view that the legal system does not have meaning independently of its wider social context.

Are there problems that you see with procedural fairness?

The significance of this question does lead me back to your really interesting observation:

'Why can't we believe victims, while also allowing a legal process to play out? It seems in part we're so steadfast in some idealised possibility of objectivity that a jury can arrive at, as though they are not shaped and influenced by their life experiences.'

It is another conflation, don't you think? Where the legal principle 'innocent until proven guilty' is divorced from its legal context, and becomes interpreted to mean 'morally correct until (legally) determined to be morally wrong'. Porter and Morrison were asking the public to take the standard of behaviour in the legal context (which lawyers know is 'beyond all reasonable doubt') as the everyday standard of social life (which is mere belief). And why shouldn't the population believe Brittany Higgins, and others, without being interpreted to mean that those whose behaviour is being criticised would be found guilty according to a court of law? As you say, surely we can have more than a singular meaning of truth – and that legal truth should not be seen as the best or only standard?

I notice that those who have been criticised for inappropriate behaviour seem to make appeals to the public and draw on this conflation when the allegations are acknowledged as having serious repercussions, particularly in terms of a person's career. Last year and recently, the issue has been sexual harassment and assault. But I have also seen it as a response to allegations of racial discrimination and harassment. To me, this appeal seems to shut down the voices of those reporting the issue, deflecting attention away from the harmful experience, and focusing instead on the harm created by the complaint. (This was driven home last year with the Attorney-General's tears – particularly as we didn't get to hear from the complainant at all.) Therefore, the person whose behaviour is being criticised becomes the more tangible, and aggrieved, victim.

What do you think contributes to the discourse that truth is legal truth, and there is just one singular truth?

she/her

> I hope you're having a good week.
>
> This relationship between law and truth has me thinking.

SAROUCHE

> The first thing I think of are the legal fictions relating to the concept of Terra Nullius, and then subsequently Native Title. The court was able to sustain a fiction that 'no one was here' for 200 years. As I see it, there's no way to escape the consequences of this. What do we make of a legal system that lies but is also the arbiter of truth? So as a foundational question of colonisation, if you ask me 'What contributes to the discourse that truth is legal truth, and that there is just one singular truth?', it was the legitimation of settler violence. This truth-making singularity that Western colonial institutions imposed was a means of legal domination and control. Of course it would then preference people in a hierarchy, from white cis-gendered men down to anyone who is willing to perform white patriarchy and settler violence.

What's particularly interesting, is that we have had subsequent waves of social change come through as attempts to take on this singularity and domination. Looking back now, it's particularly egregious that it wasn't until the early 1990s that the last Australian jurisdiction removed the marital rape exemption. But we've shifted some way in 30 years. With the passage of amendments that made same-sex marriage legal in 2017, we can view the construct of marriage as one that's progressing to a more inclusive and diverse form, even though it maintains vestiges of patriarchy, gender and hetero normativity, and obviously, monogamy. I'm raising this example to say that, well, marriage can be viewed as an oppressive structure, and yet the community has shifted its conception, for the better. So maybe we can work for structural change.

34

To re-state my answer to your question, it's power that contributes to the discourse that truth is legal truth, and that there is just one singular truth. But I'm curious about whether we should disentangle these two concepts (law and truth), or alternatively make law more truthful, by offering a diversity of standpoints to what truth could be. What do you think of that?

they them

Have you heard of the World Courts of Women? This is a movement that has global roots, of women who organise and create public hearings for women who are excluded or oppressed from traditional justice mechanisms.

You may think the fact that these courts aren't formal state courts raises questions about legitimacy and power.

But I've watched footage of these courts and they appear spaces of law and accountability to me. When we think traditionally about courts, we think about the monopoly of the state to violence, which means here to detain and imprison. Should accountability come with a framework of punishment or healing?

What's clear with our formal mechanisms is that they try to do a hodgepodge of both, and so the attempts at healing victims and offenders end up secondary to the theatre of adjudication and punishment. Can you think of concrete steps for us to improve the rules of the court and of procedural fairness to make legal processes more sympathetic to complainants and to offer healing for both victims and offenders?

Regards,

Sarouche

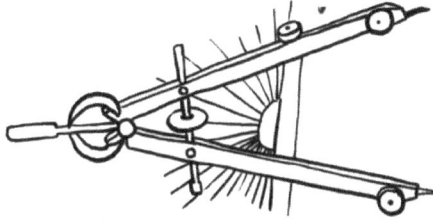

ENLIGHTENMENT HEROES WEATHERING THE ANTHROPOCENE WITH TRUTH, DISRUPTION AND CLIMATE JUSTICE.

Oh wait, the so-called 'Enlightenment' applied terra nullius to the clearly inhabited 'Australian' continent.

Hi Sarouche,

You ask a big question!

> 'Should we disentangle these two concepts (law and truth), or alternatively make law more truthful, by offering a diversity of standpoints to what truth could be?'

The relationship between law and truth is interesting and I don't know if I have an answer, so I will instead tease out some ideas that this question prompts for me. I hope this makes sense!

ANNE

I think that there are some binaries operating in law, truth and the issue of sexual assault that reinforce each other. Specifically, if an accused is held to be not-guilty of a crime, then there is an assumption that they were telling the truth. And the inverse is thought to be true; if, despite claiming innocence, the accused is found guilty of a crime by a court, then they must have been lying. But we know that this is a very simplistic picture. Just because a person is determined to be not-guilty by a court, does not mean that they are telling the truth. It is overlaying the binary of guilty/innocent with lying/truth. I wonder if the criminal standard of beyond all reasonable doubt also is at work here, being the equivalent of 'the truth' (almost).

And this is laid over another binary in crimes such as sexual assault, i.e. consent/non-consent. That is, where there is no sexual assault, there was consent. I can see why for feminist activist purposes, given the historical expectation that women always consent, it has been strategic (and important) to create a boundary line that creates the binary of consent/non-consent. And the tussle more recently has been to see that the default position is no consent, unless clearly and enthusiastically indicated otherwise. For all the great impact that this has had, it has come at the cost of making something clear when at times, the line is crossed and blurred.

I think all of these binaries were drawn upon by Christian Porter in his appeal to the public. That is, since he was not-guilty of a crime (or rather, no criminal charges could be laid as the complainant had died), he was telling the truth, and potentially that there was consent (no sexual assault). Here is a person who as a politician has power, and as the Attorney-General has legal authority, drew upon those binaries to achieve his own personal purposes, justify his actions and escape criticism. The downside is that it comes at a cost of drawing upon (personal and professional) privilege to further hide (legal) privilege. Just yuck.

And what about the legal decision-makers? If a single truth in law is a fiction (and we probably both agree on that), what narratives make that fiction seem real? I think truth in law is constructed in two main ways: who speaks the truth and by what process these people say that they arrive at the truth. In our colonial Australian system, those who speak the truth of law are judges, those who have been recognised by (more or less) their legal colleagues as being able to effectively use the process that makes decisions recognisable as law. And, the decisions that are recognisable as colonial law, are those of quasi-scientific deduction, cloaked in a language of logic, objectivity and a singular correct conclusion. And so the power of judges is denied, and their differently truthful perspectives effaced.

Perhaps it is not so much a matter of disentangling truth and law, or revising a concept of legal truth to include multiple truths, but about critically questioning the way that 'truths' are produced and whose interests the productions benefit. That way, truth (and law) is always recognised as an impossible fiction, and it ensures that multiple perspectives always have opportunities to break through should the possibilities and means of truth production become either simplistic, reified or foreclosed by one set of interests.

Because, of course, truth and how it is produced could be otherwise. And I guess I am thinking of one way of answering your question:

> 'Can you think of concrete steps for us to improve the rules of the court and of procedural fairness to make legal processes more sympathetic to complainants and to offer healing for both victims and offenders?'

For instance, is it possible to think of a legal system as one that resolves disputes without any recourse to a singular truth, that has the authority to say 'this is what happens next', or alternatively, has no authority and there is a process the parties follow through which they negotiate an outcome? Perhaps this is what the World Courts of Women offer. I wasn't aware of them so thanks for that example. They seem like another mechanism for determining disputes with a means of accountability that does not require any recourse to state power and legitimacy through appeals to truth and objectivity or 'one right answer'.

Have you heard about how new technologies and images from diverse sources are narrating the digital record around live events? It's a technological process that aims to democratise the source of lived experiences, all of which are subjective and reflect a personal and political agenda, but which when drawn together provide a rich collection of 'truths' including evidence of contestation and different ways of seeing the same event.

I hope at least some of the above made sense!

Cheers,

Anne

Anne and Sarouche are right: however, one of the most important truths we cannot overlook is evidence of the climate emergency we have had since 1938, with predictions before then.

Another truth is that I am an assault survivor.

45

I used to scratch and
pick at my scalp until
it scabbed and bled,
dermatillomania,
when I was fourteen,
otherwise keeping up
a façade that I felt had to
last until graduation.

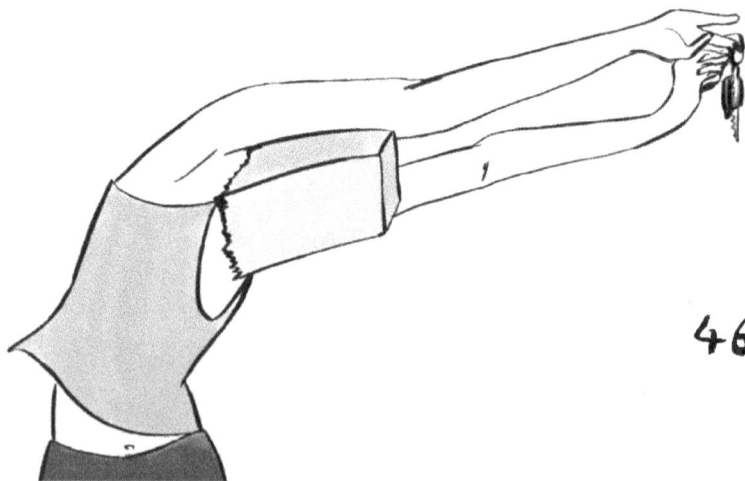

The person attacking me was also a student. He held a knife to my throat in the first surprise assault, but that was okay according to him because he revealed afterwards that it was unopened. He's a doctor these days. Which might be okay, because I always thought he was meaner when he was bored.

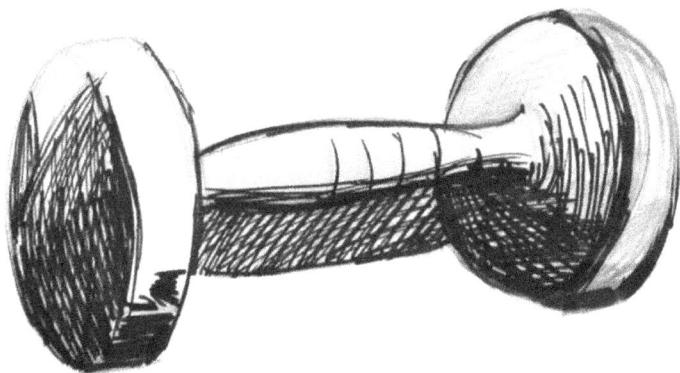

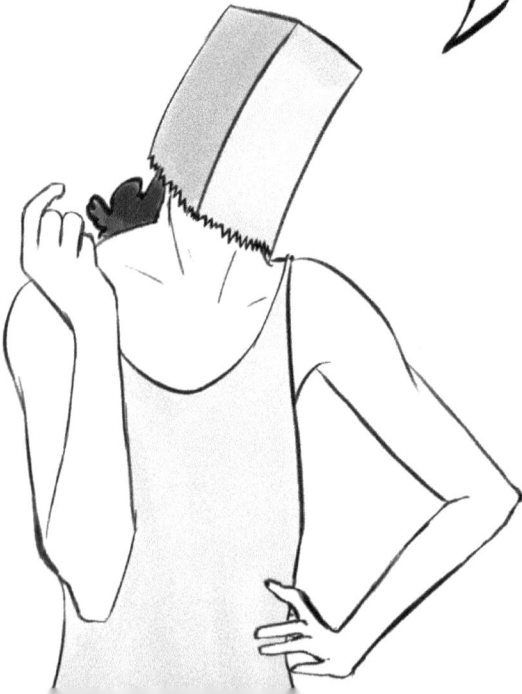

Sadly my PTSD and associated haphephobia means I can't be the romance writer climate activists keep asking of me, because I am too sarcastic.

You are stuck with us academics.

48

SAROUCHE

Hi Anne,

Thanks for offering such a layered and thoughtful response.
I see how the binaries can be used in harmful ways, and I felt
energised and hopeful when you wrote about questioning the
ways truths are produced so that:

'Truth (and law) is always recognised as an impossible fiction,
and ensuring that the multiple perspectives always have
opportunities to break through should the possibilities and
means about truth production become either simplistic, reified
or foreclosed by one set of interests.'

That's a call to action that really speaks to me.

I really like the diversifying of truth and it aligns with the scholarship I'm drawing on. In particular, ~~De Sousa Santos'~~* work about how the law treats other epistemologies, Escobar's work about the pluriversal, and Watson's work about Raw Law. I haven't spent enough time thinking about how 'the archive' has diversified in a structured way. Someone I deeply respect is a photojournalist at protests on Aboriginal justice issues, and I suppose it struck me as particularly powerful during the Greek financial crisis and the Arab Spring how technology could be used effectively to offer richer perspectives on truth and justice and as a counterpoint to control. I feel disheartened though, in both instances, by how statecraft petered out both movements. I suspect that without technology itself divesting from the concentration of power, I don't believe it can truly be an emancipatory tool.

* see W.T.A.A.F. on page 73.

For me the other component I keep returning to is how far we are from considering harm. I suppose my overall reflection is that the legal system seems to concentrate on two ideas: truth and punishment, and everything else comes second. I agree that truth-tellings are a part of healing, but they are only one part of it, and I'm not at all convinced that punishment does anything for healing. So this becomes a matter of where we turn our gaze and why. If we were to shift and focus our gaze towards harm, not necessarily looking away from truths, but remembering what we want is a society where everyone gets to heal, feel safe, and thrive, then maybe the purposes and the tools of law change too. For example, at the moment we have a system that's remedially driven to either physical punishment through detention, or to pecuniary compensation for victims. This too, could be otherwise.

If we come to your original concern, it's tragic that the primary harm in this instance was death. And I think we can observe that if the systems of justice and law were more oriented around harm, and had as its primary focus healing both victims and offenders, then I believe we would have the best chance of people like the complainant not self-harming. That's something we should all be working towards.

I'm mindful that we didn't really put parameters around our dialogue so I thought I would check where the natural conclusion might be? Let me know if you want to chat about it. I'm really grateful for the opportunity to write these thoughts out though, and I've found I've read your emails a number of times to consider and reconsider your ideas, so thank you.

Regards,

Sarouche

Hi Sarouche, I really like your incorporation of the idea of harm and healing into the conversation. And I agree, a legal system fixated on punishment or economic reparation fails dismally at addressing harm (and healing) in a meaningful way. Perhaps as Cover reminds us, the legal system is (mostly) an apparatus of state violence, and perhaps better at fulfilling the needs of those who are already privileged, than rectifying the structural (and other) injustices experienced by those who have not had a voice in the production of this system (at least to date).

ANNE

And I think it brings us back to one of the key concerns underpinning the whole scenario, and a recognition of the tragic stakes at play if the law (and other discourses) are not challenged.

Thanks also so much to you, for engaging in this interesting and thought-provoking experiment! I too, have read and re-read your emails, reflecting and pondering, and revisiting. All the things that I value most about academic life!

I think we have indeed reached a point where perhaps we can draw those threads together into something! Yes, perhaps it would be productive to chat about how we could do that? What works for you?

Cheers (and many, many, many thanks!),

Anne

EPILOGUE

I remember following the news in March 2021, as the details of various allegations about sexual harassment and assault by those who make our laws were aired. It was tragic and awful, but what struck me first was that it was unsurprising. It was unsurprising because whichever gender we identify with, we have witnessed and experienced these harms in our daily lives. In the classrooms, in our sports clubs, at restaurants, bars and in shops. Almost every day it is on TV, film and in social media.

ANNE

But the news in March 2021 had a particularly sinister tone. The very individuals and systems that were responsible for changing this reality – the Attorney-General, the Prime Minister, our elected representatives, our workplaces, laws and legal processes – had all failed so dismally to articulate the many connected issues and problems. And as an academic interested in gender and the law, I had to ask 'Why? How?'

Asking these questions out loud allowed me to find a number of wonderful, insightful and genuine scholars who were equally concerned and curious. Sarouche was one of those people. From the very beginning, his ideas about law and truth intrigued me. Exploring these questions in conversation turned out to be both a captivating way of exploring possibilities, and a helpful way to re-think issues through so many different perspectives.

I am so grateful that Sarouche and I started our conversation, one that circled and swirled, and captured in text via email over a couple of months. It was a conversation that led us, rather than one that we directed, because who knew where it would go?! And just as importantly, as it turned out, I feel as if the form of that conversation (and its graphic representation), captures and conveys those layers and connections as much as the words did.

When I first wrote to Anne last year, I remember feeling a sense of growing agitation from years of practice about how the law deals with truth. Most of my practicing life I've worked with victims of violence and I could see how the burden of proof made their encounters with the justice system horrific. And at the same time, I struggle to sit with the punishment mechanisms of the justice system. The organisation Sisters Inside, which advocates for female detainees, states:

'We believe that no one is better than anyone else. People are neither "good" nor "bad" – our environment and life circumstances play a major role in how we behave.'

SAROUCHE

To me, that's an incredibly simple and powerful premise our justice system and our society can't handle. And the majority of the empirical evidence backs it up. If people aren't good or bad, then what purpose does punishment serve?

If we look at the profile of people in prison – about 1 in 3 people in prison are Aboriginal and Torres Strait Islander, while 3 in 100 people in Australia are Aboriginal and Torres Strait Islander. It starts to look like prison is another place which manifests colonial violence.

Having said this, I want to contrast this with the circumstances around the events Anne highlighted last year. In one instance, violence against women literally in the national halls of power and an incredibly cruel and incompetent workplace response. And in another instance, the premier legal officer of the country did not see it fit to stand aside while serious allegations were being aired which would inherently hamper his ability to administer the legal system. These circumstances were unacceptable, and yet faced with a system of justice that is unable to deliver justice, what were we meant to do?

they/ them

I felt Anne's invitation a powerful response to the agitation I've been feeling in all of this. When we eventually met together and came up with the idea of a series of emails to one another, it felt novel, and yet dialogue is one of the oldest methods of learning, isn't it? Looking back on the piece now, the key tension we circled around is the relationship between law and truth, and the methodological problem we encounter in this system is singularity.

So it seemed like conducting dialogue outside of singularity is already constructing an otherwise, and I like that. Indeed, Anne's call to action about allowing multiple perspectives to break through as a counterpoint to particular interests that law often served was so powerful.

And as a method of learning, I can say I'd receive Anne's emails with trepidation and excitement. I'd allow her thoughts to sit with me through multiple reads, I'd construct and re-construct a response. It felt more authentic than what we often see in learning. I wasn't interested in prosecuting an argument, or disagreeing with Anne (not just because I was agreeing with her!). I wanted our ideas to stay open and curious, and see what shape our work would take. What I liked most was that it didn't take the pathway that I expected, and that made the exchange richer.

When we met afterwards and discussed how we would give our dialogue an audience, it was exciting that we both kept pushing against singularity and decided to explore a visual format. I thought of the graphic novels I've read and how much of an affective medium it is. Having seen Kirsten's work now, without a doubt her vision layers another dimension to our dialogue and I'm grateful for this.

My final thought comes from Arundhati Roy's engagement on singularity, where she repurposes the words of John Berger and tells us:

'"Never again will a single story be told as though it's the only one." There can never be a single story. There are only ways of seeing.'

'That's the end?! Are you serious? Keep going! We have so many questions!'

Finality is the enemy of the kind of hustler storytelling I do that gives people reasons to keep my climate activist friends and I out of jail.

See you next time for more things I tried to avoid talking about. Maybe ex-Justice Heydon being found out for sexual harassment in 2020. Apparently it was an open secret and no one did anything earlier.

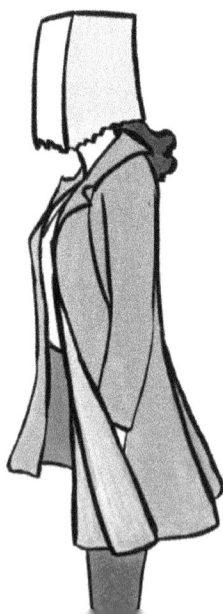

66

Kirsten

Sarouche

How do you both feel about a new ending to the novel? At the conference people spoke about leaning into our identities in the work. I think this could be a good way to end the novel (how meta, right!). I remember the first time I wrote to you Anne, I was concerned about taking up space as a cis-gendered male. I feel though, and particularly now that I have a son, that I have a responsibility to fight against gender injustice.

The other thing is that in this work we are drawing a clear link between gender injustice and colonisation which raises important questions. In my identity, I am both an oppressed person and an oppressor: I am a Muslim, Afghan-Iranian-Australian, cis-gendered male, who lives on stolen land as a settler. I experience daily encounters of racism and I feel the psychological pressure of epistemic violence, but I also own property in the Torrens title system, my passport allows me to cross borders without issue, I walk city alleyways at night with a relative ease that only men have and my education and opportunities have allowed material and influential power. I am a liminal identity, but it is both my experiences of power and dispower, and the interaction between them, that offer possibilities of re-imagining justice. The ambivalence of my situation, to quote Burrows (2004, 11-12), 'signifies that a person can experience oppositional emotions that co-exist and can remain in fluctuating opposition to each other ... Contradictory ideas / emotions / wishes transgress and disrupt polar opposites that idealize fixity and closure.' What's powerful about this state of ambivalence is that it's not a call to the inaction that is so central to those with power in modernity. Rather, as Milatovic (2015, 3) says, it's an invitation to dialogue, engagement, and social action. So for me, when we are considering the question of justice we should consider our own privilege as part of it, and rather than not taking up space, we should instead think about how we take up space and how much space we take up.

Another great question — how to end? I guess that is the unsatisfying thing about a conversation, or a good story, that they cannot resolve all the threads of ideas. But the threads are useful too. They spark future imaginings and re-imaginings of the conversation — sequels and spin offs even! But I agree that articulating how our lived experiences inform our ideas and interests helps us to be honest about what we have noticed, said, avoided or ignored. Like Sarouche, but differently, parts of my identity are privileged whilst others aren't. Today, I could describe myself as a cis-gendered, able-bodied, heterosexual, white woman, who lives on First Nations land and has inherited the economic benefits arising from colonialism and the environmental degradation of the planet. The English racial and cultural privilege of my parents meant that they were able to travel to Australia without restrictions in the 1950s and 60s. They were welcomed migrants, and by accident, Australia became the land of my birth. Yet I habitually feel the micro (and sometimes macro) aggressions of structural gender violence. I like to choose where I walk, but there are annoying internal voices which remind me to walk faster, have a backup plan, or take my dogs. I have had access to a quality education in a profession of status and privilege, although that environment also reminds me daily of my working class family background. Perhaps a mutual awareness of the shifting privileges that attach to some of our identities but not others, explains why Sarouche and I started a conversation about truth, law and justice in the first place. But I am not sure that it is possible to explain all the ways that I am for the purposes of standpoint theory, or indeed, if I should. In addition to the blind spots that come with privilege and the identities that I unconsciously perform that benefit me in ways I am not aware of (yet) and can't identify (a reader might legitimately do that for me!), ambivalent identities have potential too. While the power to hide an identity is unevenly distributed amongst identities, lives and spaces, disclosing only glimpses of our identity can also generate imaginative new possibilities about what we say. Maybe the diverse ways of being 'read' are an important part of what (and how much) we say?

Kirsten

I hope that what we have created so far is not too cryptic. If things have been left open, unresolved or surreal, this is a philosophical reality for us.

I am an able-bodied white person living on First Nations land, with a good education. Despite working to mitigate the climate emergency in a way I would describe as combative, I get complacent.

Abusers of power arise in areas I thought had inoculated themselves against the patriarchy. There is no such thing as a 'safe' space: saying so is making a promise that cannot be kept. Spaces can and should aspire to be 'safer.'

W.T.A.F.! I imagine that you've both been following the Lehrmann trial and you've heard that it was abandoned right at the very end, during the jury's deliberations? Apparently, it was because one of the jurors went against the court's directions not to conduct outside research, and brought in a few academic research papers to share with the other jurors. Can you believe that one of these 'research' papers, of all things, discussed the prevalence of false complaints about sexual assaults? It feels like this tragic conclusion to the trial captures everything about law, truth and violence that we have been thinking about. It is yet another example of the law (and its systems) failing individuals who are asking it to make a decision about sexual violence, whether the accused is convicted or not. And not only that, the way the law has failed spectacularly seems to do so in a manner that has undermined (again) the ability of women to speak the truth about harms done to them. Since the issue doesn't seem to be resolved, and the same things keep happening over and over – do you get the feeling that we're stuck in Groundhog Day? This makes finding a place to end this conversation and publish our work seem impossible. Perhaps we will just have to leave the work unresolved and incomplete, as things are in life? I guess it also means that we can promise readers sequels?

Anne

W.T.A.A.F.?!? In 2023 various and separate allegations of sexual harassment were made against De Sousa Santos. At least from 2018, graffiti appeared on the walls of the University of Coimbra where De Sousa Santos taught. The graffiti says 'Out Boaventura, we all know.' He has been stood down while an investigation takes place. The stories of the women who have come forward are deeply distressing and also allege an institutional culture of knowing complicity. We discovered this story in the final stages of writing our novel and it affected us profoundly because it speaks to the issues we are writing about and because De Sousa Santos' work has been a companion against many of the injustices we see in law. We don't think it's authentic to deny the role that De Sousa Santos has played in our work, but at the same time we want to draw attention to the women who have come forward. Bella Gonçalves, one of the complainants and now a legislator in Brazil, stated: 'The violence that I suffered led to even more violent processes. That's why I stayed silent for so long.'

Sarouche

ANTIFA FORA BOAVENTURA TODAS SABEMOS

Glossary of Key Terms in Once upon a time in Australia

Summary

1. Christian Porter and the events surrounding his resignation:

Christian Porter was the Federal Attorney-General 2017-2021 and a member of the Liberal Party, representing the people of Pearce from 2013-2022. In 2021 an allegation of rape against a Minister was reported by the ABC, but the identity of the Minister was not revealed. The woman who made the allegation wrote a statement in 2019, and commenced a complaint with the NSW Police in 2020, but took her life shortly after. The NSW Police closed their investigation. Then in 2021, a friend wrote an anonymous letter including the woman's statement setting out the allegations, and sent the letter to a number of Members of Parliament. When Mr Porter was identified as the person at the centre of the allegations, there were calls for a public inquiry but the Prime Minister refused. Porter refused to resign and in a televised press conference suggested that doing so would imperil the justice system. He stated:

> 'If I stand down from my position as Attorney-General because of an allegation about something that simply did not happen, then any person in Australia can lose their career, their job, their life's work, based on nothing more than an accusation that appears in print.
>
> If that happens, anyone in public life is able to be removed simply by the printing of an allegation. Every child we raise can have their lives destroyed by online reporting of accusations alone. My guess is that if I were to resign and that set a new standard, there wouldn't be much need for an Attorney-General anyway, because there would be no rule of law left to protect in this country. So I will not be part of letting that happen while I am Attorney-General and I am sure that you will ask, so I will state to you, I am not standing down or aside.'

Christian Porter was eventually moved to a different portfolio and did not seek to recontest his seat in the 2022 election. Porter also started defamation proceedings against the ABC and the ABC journalist who produced the story. The claim was eventually withdrawn and no damages were awarded. Part of the legal fees were paid by a blind trust with funds from an anonymous source.

2. Australia's #MeToo movement:

The MeToo movement is a global movement that from 2017 onwards, used Twitter and other social media platforms to highlight the seriousness and magnitude of gender-based and sexual violence. While starting in the United States in response to Harvey Weinstein, the movement gained prominence around the world. In Australia a number of events brought the issue to national attention, including:

- The ABC 4 corners documentary 'Bursting the Canberra Bubble'
- The #letherspeak campaign by sexual assault survivor Grace Tame, which sought to change the *Evidence Act* in Tasmania that prohibited the publication of material that identified survivors of sexual assault

- The allegation made by former Liberal Party staffer, Brittany Higgins, that she was raped inside Parliament House by Bruce Lehrmann and the government response to it
- The reporting of the rape allegation made against Christian Porter and the government response to it
- The 2020 investigation into the multiple allegations of sexual assault by former High Court Justice Dyson Heydon
- The 2020 report by the Sex Discrimination Commissioner, Kate Jenkins, entitled 'Respect@Work', which was a national review of workplace sexual harassment with 55 recommendations for systemic reform, and the subsequent 2021 report by Commissioner, entitled 'Set the Standard', which looked at sexual harassment in the Australian Parliament.

3. The toughening of protest laws across Australia:

While it is commonly accepted that there is a right to free speech in Australia, this has a limited basis in law. Whilst Australia is a signatory to the *ICCPR*, which includes a right to freedom of expression (article 19(2)) and a right to peaceful assembly (article 21), these obligations have not been incorporated explicitly into domestic law. The strongest protection of protest is through the implied constitutional freedom of political expression. However, there are significant restrictions placed on this constitutional freedom, including its nexus with politics and elections, and the ability of the government to proportionally infringe this freedom for a legitimate reason. As a consequence, there is no general legal right to protest in Australia. Indeed, most of Australia's jurisdictions have legislation which regulates protest activities. These laws have become increasingly restrictive through the requirements of notification and approval for use of certain public spaces. Even should permission be given, various criminal laws continue to operate during a protest. These restrictions are increasingly justified on the basis of protecting public safety, but the threat of criminal prosecution for not complying with 'move along' laws, or for trespassing and disturbing the peace and/or traffic offences, raises the stakes for those involved in protests. Most recently, there has been a move in many jurisdictions towards increased sentences and harsher bail conditions for such offences (see *Roads and Crimes Amendment Act 2022* (NSW)).

These laws have resulted in a number of particularly harsh sentences handed out to NSW climate change protesters who disrupted traffic on Sydney Harbour Bridge on 13 April 2022. Human rights agencies have been particularly critical of such laws: <https://www.hrw.org/news/2022/06/22/australia-climate-protesters-rights-violated>. The jurisdictions of Victoria and Tasmania are currently considering toughening their protest laws further.

4 Australia's refugee laws since Tampa:

Since the enactment of the *Australian Constitution* in 1901, the Commonwealth Parliament has the power to pass laws relating to migration and immigration. This power has been interpreted widely, allowing the Executive wide discretion in determining which migrants may enter Australia, as well as a wide discretion to revoke permission of migrants to remain in the country, and subsequently deport them. Refugees can be described as 'forced migrants', fleeing their home countries out of fear of persecution. There are a number of international conventions which create obligations in relation to the treatment and acceptance of refugees, to which Australia is a signatory. Australia has experienced many waves of refugees arriving at its borders, and over time has had many different policies that have sought to balance its international obligations with its desire to exercise control over its territorial borders.

The *Tampa* incident occurred on 24 August 2001 and marked a contemporary and particularly punitive approach to refugee policy and border protection in Australia. The *Tampa* was a Norwegian cargo ship which had rescued a number of refugees from a sinking Indonesian fishing boat in the Indian Ocean. The Norwegian ship sought permission to dock in Australia and disembark its passengers, some of whom were in poor health. Although the Australian government had denied permission to enter Australian waters, on 29 August the Captain of the *Tampa* entered anyway. On doing so, a number of military personnel boarded the ship and took control. The government response described the incident as a 'border protection' crisis and justified the Liberal government passing a number of sweeping laws on border control and national security. With the bombing of the US trade towers just two weeks after this incident, public approval of the Liberal government's management of the crisis soared, arguably contributing to the re-election of the Liberal government to Parliament in November 2001 for another term. It also gave the Liberal government a mandate for a number of internationally criticised refugee policies, including a number of policies to prevent the arrival of refugees in Australia like the 'Pacific Solution'.

5. The Western Legal Tradition

One of the most significant impacts of colonisation has been the imposition of European legal and political structures on other cultures and nations. The legal system, as it has been traditionally taught in English-speaking countries, imagines a legal system with the traditions of common law, and a legal system with the traditions of civil law. Common law is the system under which most English-speaking jurisdictions operate, and is understood as a system where law is made by judges through the application of precedent in adversarial, oral hearings. As countries are governed increasingly through legislation, statutes have become the primary ways laws are made in this system. Of course there are a myriad of other legal systems but the colonial power of these two traditions has meant that they hold epistemological power as legal systems of thought.

6. The 2021 March 4 Justice

The protest of 15 March 2021 was instigated by Janine Hendry in response to the failure of the Australian government to respond adequately to a number of issues relating to sexual harassment and assault. (<https://www.smh.com.au/national/it-was-a-visceral-anger-the-tweet-that-spawned-nationwide-protests-20210311-p579uk.html>).

Issues which had been circulating in the media included; the allegation by Brittany Higgins that she had been raped as a parliamentary staffer, the failure of the government to launch an inquiry into the allegation against the Attorney-General Christian Porter, and the failure to respond to a damning report by Commissioner Kate Jenkins on the extent of sexual harassment at work (See entry #14 below). Organisers claim that over 110,000 people marched in support of gender equality in Australia. The marches were held in all Australian States and Territories, including at Commonwealth Parliament House in Canberra. The organisers made four key demands in a petition to the government:

1. Full independent investigations into all cases of gendered violence and timely referrals to appropriate authorities. Full public accountability for findings.
2. Fully implement the 55 recommendations in the Australian Human Rights Commission's Respect@Work report of the National Inquiry into Sexual Harassment in Australian Workplaces 2020.
3. Lift public funding for gendered violence prevention to world's best practice.
4. The enactment of a federal *Gender Equality Act* to promote gender equality. It should include a gender equity audit of parliamentary practices.

See <https://www.march4justice.org.au/>.

7. The death of Eurydice Dixon

Eurydice Dixon was killed by Jaymes Todd in Melbourne's Princes Park in June 2018. Her death sparked protests and national attention in Australia concerning women's safety. Dixon was a comedian and actor and had been walking home from a performance when she was raped and killed by Todd.

8. Brittany Higgins and the trial of Bruce Lehrmann

Brittany Higgins was a junior Liberal staffer working for Commonwealth Senator Linda Reynolds. After attending an evening work function in March 2019, she returned to Parliament House with colleague Bruce Lehrmann to Senator Reynolds' office. That night at the office she claims that she was raped by Mr Lehrmann, slipping in and out of consciousness. She was found in the office by security guards the next morning, naked and disorientated. Senator Reynolds subsequently became aware of the incident but does not seem to have undertaken any investigation and is claimed to have provided only limited support to Ms Higgins. Ms Higgins did not involve ACT police at the time. After resigning as a staffer in November 2020, she raised her complaints within the Liberal Party again, but they were ignored. On 15 February 2021, Ms Higgins went to the media with her complaint, which followed hot on the heels of the news about Attorney-General Mr Porter and former High Court Justice Dyson Heydon. The news sparked an outpouring of frustration and nationwide protests. Ms Higgins appeared as a speaker at the March 4 Justice in Canberra.

Following the media attention, the Liberal government under (former) Prime Minister Scott Morrison instigated an inquiry into parliamentary culture (see Jenkins Review at #14 below). Mr Morrison and Ms Reynolds issued a public apology to Ms Higgins. The incident was referred to ACT police, and Mr Bruce

Lehrmann was charged with sexual assault. Mr Lehrmann pleaded not guilty, and a trial was held in the ACT Supreme Court in October 2022. When the trial ended and the jury was considering the verdict, it was discovered that one of the jurors had disobeyed a judicial direction not to refer to any literature outside that which was considered in the trial. The juror had brought into the jury deliberations two articles on the prevalence of false allegations in sexual assault trials. Following this discovery, the trial was abandoned. Subsequently, there was much media attention on whether another trial would be held. In December 2022, the ACT Director of Public Prosecutions reported that it had dropped the charges against Mr Lehrmann. Reasons reported by the media included the risk to Ms Higgins' life. Subsequently, problems with the evidence gathered by ACT police were also reported. Since then, Ms Higgins has come to a settlement with the Commonwealth for a confidential sum.

9. Latin Maxims and how they are used in legal judgement:

In the English common law, a judge can draw on the rules as set out in previous cases. This is the system of precedent. Whether or not the judge must follow a particular rule expounded in a previous case depends (mostly) on whether that case is binding. For a judge, a decision of a court that is higher in the 'same' court hierarchy is binding. The rule from a decision of a court at the same or lower level in the same hierarchy, or from a different hierarchy, is persuasive at best. In Australia there are different hierarchies in the Federal, State and Territory legal systems. However, the High Court of Australia is currently the highest and final court in the Australian hierarchy.

Aside from these sources, judges rely on other notions including principles of Canonical law that have been absorbed the common law, as well as Latin maxims, which are principles of Old Roman law. An example of this is 'de minimus non curat lex', which translates as 'the law does not concern itself with trifles', meaning, if a matter is inconsequential, the law should not concern itself with those matters.

10. Judges' directions to juries and jury objectivity to hear evidence:

It has been an important principle of British law that criminal trials are held before a jury. A jury is a group of individuals who are selected from members of the community. The purpose of a jury trial is to ensure the acceptability of the criminal justice system through involving the participation of the community. The jury trial also ensures that the verdict is delivered by the defendant's 'peers' and not just a person in authority.

Given the use of members of the community, the judge's role includes explaining the law and the relevance of evidence in criminal trials to the jury. A judge may give a direction, or a warning, to explain: the meaning or interpretation of an aspect of the law, the relevance of evidence that has been presented, or how the evidence may be used (or not used) to answer legal questions. The content of the directions and warnings has emerged from decisions in previous cases, and are now often included in judge bench books in most jurisdictions. More recently, legislative amendments in some jurisdictions also now require some directions to be given in particular situations; for e.g. *Juries Directions Act 2015* (Vic).

There is a general expectation that a jury will decide on the basis of the evidence offered during the hearing rather than relying on outside sources. This is considered to align with procedural fairness because the value of the evidence of outside sources was not able to be tested by the parties during the hearing. This direction was given to the jury in the trial of Bruce Lehrmann (see entry #8 above).

The directions (and warnings) given by a judge are intended to dispel common cultural norms or expectations where they depart from the law. The use of directions has expanded recently, particularly in the case of sexual assault trials. For instance, a judge might direct a jury about the law of consent and reasonable belief, or that certain aspects of a person's appearance or conduct does not amount to consent. These directions explicitly combat social myths about the relevance of certain facts to the issue of consent such as: wearing revealing clothing, acting flirtatiously, going to the accused's home, not saying no, and/or not refusing vigorously or loudly enough.

11. Jury representation:

The composition of juries is a fundamental question of justice. For example, in a number of Australian jurisdictions it was only in the 1960s that women were permitted to serve on juries and only in the 1970s that formal discrimination was removed. The composition of juries with respect to Indigenous peoples is a particularly salient issue in Australia given the context of colonisation. In the Northern Territory, which has the highest Indigenous population proportionate to the non-Indigenous community, there is a gross underrepresentation of Indigenous peoples in criminal law juries. There were no Aboriginal jurors in the murder trial of Zachary Rolfe, a Northern Territory police officer who shot and killed an Aboriginal man (see entry #13 below).

12. Hannah McGlade:

Hannah McGlade CF is an Australian academic, human rights advocate and lawyer. She is a Kurin Minang Noongar woman of the Bibulman nation. She is currently an associate professor at Curtin University's law school. Her research focuses on justice for First Nations Australians with a focus on women and children. Her recent research includes:

Hannah McGlade, 'Aboriginal women and the Commonwealth Government's response to Mabo—an international human rights perspective' In *Words and Silences.* (Routledge, 2020) 139-156.

Hannah McGlade, 'Australia's treatment of Indigenous prisoners: the continuing nature of human rights violations in West Australian jail cells' In Berghs, Maria, et al., (eds) *The Routledge handbook of disability activism.* (Routledge, 2019) 274.

13. The Trial of Zachary Rolfe and the death of Kumanjayi Walker:

Kumanjayi Walker was a 19-year-old Aboriginal man who was shot and killed by Northern Territory police officer Zachary Rolfe during an attempt to arrest him in the community of Yuendumu. Rolfe had also been armed with a taser. Significantly, Walker fell over after he was shot the first time, and then Rolfe shot him twice more into his torso.

Following his death there was a community uproar, both in Yuendumu and nationally, and prosecutors decided to charge Rolfe with murder. Rolfe pleaded not guilty and was granted bail.

The jury was all white except for one juror of Asian descent. Within the procedural rules in the Northern Territory two challenges can be made to remove potential jurors, and Rolfe's defence lawyers had removed people of colour in their challenges. Rolfe was acquitted unanimously by the jury as not guilty.

During the Coronial inquest that followed, much evidence was heard about a series of racist texts that Rolfe sent during his time as a Northern Territory police officer.

Kumanjayi is a substitute name for many Aboriginal Western Desert peoples to identify them without stating their birth name.

14. The Jenkins Review:

Following the press coverage of Brittany Higgins' complaints, on 5 March 2021 the Australian government asked the Australian Human Rights Commission to conduct an independent inquiry. Led by Sex Discrimination Commissioner Kate Jenkins, the inquiry was asked to make recommendations 'to ensure that Commonwealth parliamentary workplaces are safe and respectful and that the nation's Parliament reflects best practice in prevention and response to bullying, sexual harassment and sexual assault'. The report was tabled on 30 November 2021 as 'Set the Standard: Report on the Independent Review into Commonwealth Parliamentary Workplaces' (2021)
<https://humanrights.gov.au/set-standard-2021>.

The report gathered evidence and testimony from over 900 submissions. It found that 33% of respondents had experienced sexual harassment in the parliamentary workplace. The report set out 28 recommendations as a part of the report, which attempted to create a roadmap to change the culture of government workplaces. A number of government departments have explicitly adopted the recommendations, including the Department of Finance.

15. The Rule of Law:

The concept of 'the rule of law' is familiar to many legal systems. Within the English Legal Tradition, the rule of law captures the idea that no person is above the law. This is a particularly powerful idea that requires those who make the laws, to also abide by those laws. Therefore the concept of the rule of law is also linked to equality as it follows then that every person must be treated equally under the law.

The rule of law has been used to justify very different features used in different legal systems, which means that the boundaries of the concept are somewhat ambiguous and unclear. For instance, it has been used to justify the principle of constitutional separation of powers, where no institution which makes or applies the law has all the power. That is, each branch of government (the legislature, the judiciary and the executive) provides checks and balances on the powers of the other branches. It has also been used to justify the principle of 'innocent until proven guilty'. These ideas are connected because it is accepted that only a court should determine how the law applies to an individual and whether they ought to be punished, rather than being tried and potentially punished by non-legal institutions such as the government, or even through public opinion.

Critical legal theorists have challenged the concept as a fiction, hiding the machinery of power which works to entrench inequality. For instance, Desmond Manderson in *Kangaroo Courts and the Rule of Law* (Routledge, 2012) argues that the application of the rule of law in the British colonies such as Australia failed to treat all the population equally before the law. Those with the power to create the law also continue to evade the full reach of the law, drawing upon resources and sources of privilege which enable them to use the structural inequalities within the law in their favour.

16. Rates of incarceration of Aboriginal and Torres Strait Islanders in Australia:

The high rates of incarceration of Aboriginal and Torres Strait Islanders in Australia has been well studied. The Australian Law Reform Commission in 2018 'Pathways to Justice' (<https://www.alrc.gov.au/publication/pathways-to-justice-inquiry-into-the-incarceration-rate-of-aboriginal-and-torres-strait-islander-peoples-alrc-report-133/>) reported that the Indigenous population was disproportionately represented in the prison system. Whereas Indigenous Australians represent 2% of the Australian adult population, Indigenous Australians represent 27% of the adult prison population. The fastest growing prison population is Indigenous women, who are 19 times more likely to be in prison than non-Indigenous women. Once Indigenous peoples are in the criminal justice system, they can be caught in a cycle of incarceration that can be difficult to break.

There are many reasons for the over-incarceration of Aboriginal and Torres Strait Islanders. Social inequalities arising from a history of colonisation and cultural bias expose the Indigenous population to over-policing and law enforcement. Indigenous persons are in prison for petty offences such as unpaid fines, abusive language and resisting arrest. Mandatory sentencing regimes in many Australian jurisdictions also contribute to over-representation.

17 The Rules of Procedural Fairness:

The ideal of procedural fairness is set out in common law and statutes. These rules include things like the right to be heard and to have a fair hearing, the right to be presumed innocent, the right for rules to be applied equally, the rule against bias, and notice when a decision is being made that will have an impact on an affected person.

What is deemed fair, however, is highly subjective.

18. Bail and bail conditions:

When a person has been charged with a criminal offence, the accused will usually be held by the police in custody in a 'holding cell'. As soon as possible, the accused should be taken before a judicial officer in order to determine whether they are eligible for bail. In other words, they are free to live in the community until the matter is heard. The alternative is keeping the accused in custody until the hearing. A number of factors are considered by the judicial officer in determining whether bail should be granted, and these are set out in State and Territory legislation.

In the ACT, the *Bail Act* sets out a range of factors to consider, including: the seriousness of the offence, the likelihood of absconding or interfering with the investigation of the crime, and the likelihood of reoffending, etc. (See Section 22, *Bail Act 1992* (ACT)). Bail can be granted with a range of conditions, including paying a sum of money into court as security, restrictions on movement and/ or directions to attend health treatment, etc. (See Section 24 *Bail Act 1992* (ACT)).

19. Hart:

HLA Hart was a British legal philosopher. He was an academic at Oxford University from the 1950s. His book, *The Concept of Law*, is considered one of the most important books of legal philosophy in the Western tradition. In his book, drawing on observation and ideas from cultural anthropology, he theorised that the legal system was not a set of sanctions, but rather a system of primary and secondary rules. Hart says a primary rule governs conduct (an example our authors provide is 'don't catch more fish than you need to survive'), and secondary rules govern the procedural methods by which primary rules are recognised as law, changed and adjudicated. His theoretical position about law has been described as positivism. He argues that although the law may reflect moral content, there is no specific moral content in law. A law is a law if it is recognised as such by the secondary rules.

This conceptualisation was the basis of a strong debate between Hart and Fuller. Fuller argued that without any moral content, the legal system can be co-opted by any tyrant and evil rules can be legitimised as law. This debate was published in the Harvard Law Review. See:

HLA Hart, 'Positivism and the Separation of Law and Morals' (1959) 71(4) *Harvard Law Review*, 593.

Lon L Fuller, 'Positivism and Fidelity – A Reply to Professor Hart' (1959) 71(4) *Harvard Law Review*, 593.

20. Fuller:

Lon Fuller was an American legal theorist and a contemporary of HLA Hart. In his later years, he was a Professor of Jurisprudence at Harvard. He is best known for his book, *The Morality of Law*. In it he criticised legal positivism and instead defended a secular version of natural law. That is, instead of the content of law being derived from religious doctrines, the content of law to be recognised as such, must comply with a secular and procedural form of morality. This was the inner morality of law, without which, the law could not be called law and there was no obligation to obey it.

According to Fuller, there are eight conditions that need to exist in order for a law to count as law. They are: 'The rules must be (1) sufficiently general, (2) publicly promulgated, (3) prospective (i.e., applicable only to future behaviour, not past), (4) at least minimally clear and intelligible, (5) free of contradictions, (6) relatively constant, so that they don't continuously change from day to day, (7) possible to obey, and (8) administered in a way that does not wildly diverge from their obvious or apparent meaning'. see: Lon L. Fuller, *The Morality of Law* (rev. ed. New Haven CT: Yale University Press, 1969) 33-38.

The debate between Fuller and Hart was published in the Harvard Law Review. (See entry #19 above.)

21. Legal Positivism:

Legal positivism is a tradition of jurisprudence, which put simply, suggests that the law is what authorities have decided the law to be. While this might seem obvious and tautologous there are implications and consequences in this framing. It recognises law as a social construct, and implicates jurists as people whose role is to apply a code and realise a system, rather than to interpret the ethics of what is just or fair. That system operates within its own hermetic space and allows rules to be applied within a predetermined logic.

22. Natural Law

Natural law theory generally maintains that the content of law is derived from 'natural' sources. Historically in the Western legal tradition, the natural source has been the principles of divine justice as determined by God. More recently, natural law theory was reimagined through the work of Lon Fuller. (See entry #20 above.)

23. Innocent until proven guilty:

The presumption of innocence is a principle that a person must be presumed innocent until they are proven guilty by a court of law. It is a foundational principle in many legal systems, and in Australia it is set out in the common law, statutes and international law.

24. Sexual discrimination and harassment

In Australia, legislation prohibits sex discrimination. At the Commonwealth level, the *Sex Discrimination Act 1984* (Cth) prohibits sex discrimination in a number of spheres of public life, including education, employment, provision of services, accommodation, etc. The definition of discrimination includes less favourable treatment. It can include direct discrimination (where there is intent), and indirect discrimination, which arises due to the implementation of a neutral policy in less favourable ways. There are a number of exceptions in the SDA, for instance in relation to religious groups. Complaints under the SDA are lodged and investigated through the Australian Human Rights Commission. However, the AHRC cannot make any legally enforceable determinations as a result of a complaint. This can only be achieved through taking a complaint to court.

Sexual harassment is a form of sex discrimination. It is prohibited as a form of less favourable treatment. It is defined as including an unwelcome sexual advance, a request for sexual favours, or unwelcome conduct of a sexual nature. As with sex discrimination more broadly, it is prohibited in a number of spheres of public life.

Many States and Territories have anti-discrimination (including sexual harassment) legislation, including on the basis of sex, sexual identity, pregnancy, etc. An individual can choose the forum in which to lodge a complaint. Some States and Territories also protect equality on the basis of sex through Human Rights legislation.

There is much research literature critical of the effectiveness of Australia's legislative provisions and approaches to prohibiting sex discrimination and sexual harassment. For a selection, see Margaret Thornton, Beth Gaze, etc.

25. Sexual assault

Sexual assault refers to a range of different sexual criminal offences. These can range from physical acts such as touching, kissing, penetration, to showing indecent images to another person. It occurs if consent has not been given. In certain circumstances, consent cannot be given, such as when the person is underage. In the criminal law, it may be broken down to a range of specific offences including: a sexual act, sexual touching, sexual assault, and aggravated sexual assault.

For criminal offences including sexual assault, the Department of Public Prosecution decides whether to prosecute an offender. To be found guilty of an offence, it must be shown that it is 'beyond all reasonable doubt' that the offender committed the offence. As a private litigant in a civil law suit, it needs to be established on the balance of probabilities (i.e. that it is more likely it happened than it did not).

26. Racial discrimination

In Australia, legislation prohibits discrimination on the basis of race. At the Commonwealth level, the *Race Discrimination Act* (Cth) prohibits discrimination on the basis of race and ensures racial equality in a number of spheres of public life, including education, employment, provision of services, accommodation, etc. The definition of discrimination includes less favourable treatment. It can include direct discrimination (where there is intent), and indirect discrimination, which arises due to the implementation of a neutral policy in less favourable ways.

There are exceptions in the *Racial Discrimination Act 1975* (Cth) (RDA), for instance, there are exceptions for 'special measures' under section 8(1). Complaints under the RDA can be lodged with and investigated by the Australian Human Rights Commission (AHRC). However, the AHRC cannot make any legally enforceable determinations as a result of a complaint. These can only be achieved through taking a complaint to court.

Racial vilification is a form of race discrimination. Section 18C of the RDA defines racial vilification as language that is reasonably likely to offend, insult, humiliate or intimidate on the basis of someone's race, colour, or national or ethnic origin. Only vilifying comments that are made 'in public' are unlawful. A number of defences are designed to balance the prohibition against racial vilification with a protection of freedom of speech (see s18D RDA). These defences cover statements that are considered a fair comment, a fair and accurate report, an artistic work, or a statement made for a genuine purpose in the public interest.

Many States and Territories have anti-discrimination (including racial vilification) legislation, including on the basis of racial, cultural and sometimes religious identity. An individual can choose the forum in which to lodge a complaint. Some States and Territories also protect equality on the basis of race through Human Rights legislation.

There is much research literature critical of the effectiveness of Australia's legislative provisions and approaches to prohibiting race discrimination. For a selection, see Margaret Thornton, Beth Gaze, etc.

27 Terra Nullius:

When the British asserted sovereignty over what is called Australia, they did so on the basis that the land was 'Terra Nullius' or vacant. In other words, the legal fiction was that the territory now called Australia was empty when it was discovered. This fiction operated despite the clear presence of peoples living on the territory. Mental gymnastics and racial prejudice operated to rationalise the fact that although there were people on the land, they were not using the land productively (for instance through European extractive farming or fences or buildings), and so the British could validly assert their claim to legal occupation of the land according to international law.

28. Native Title:

Native Title is the legislative device currently used in Australia to recognise the continuing association of its First Nations people with the land. It was a device introduced following the landmark case of *Mabo (No 2) v Queensland*. (See entry #29.) Following the judicial recognition of Native Title through the decision of *Mabo*, the Australian government moved to pass legislation to regulate the recognition of Indigenous claims over land in Australia. It achieved this through the *Native Title Act 1992* (Cth). This act set up criteria through which Native Title could be recognised, claims could be made and acknowledged, and a Native Title

Tribunal to determine the claims. The *Native Title Act*, including its subsequent amendments, has been heavily criticised for its restrictive criteria and processes, which has made it practically difficult for many First Nations peoples to successfully pursue claims. At present, of 575 applications for recognition of Native Title heard by the NNTT, 102 have been determined to have no claim. 473 applications have led to a recognition of Native Title, either over all or part of the claimed area.

For statistics see: <http://www.nntt.gov.au/Pages/Statistics.aspx>.

29. Mabo:

In a legal context 'Mabo' usually refers to the case of *Mabo v Queensland (No 2)* 175 CLR 1, decided on 3 June 1992. After decades of advocacy, this case was the first time the High Court recognised that Aboriginal and Torres Strait Islanders had pre-colonial land interests. The interests of Indigenous peoples in the land which survived colonisation are now recognised in the form of Native Title. Native Title is now recognised over about a third of Australia's landmass. In *Mabo* the court rejected the doctrine of Terra Nullius (See entry #27 above). The court held that where Indigenous peoples could demonstrate a continuous connection to the land, they could claim a 'beneficial usufructuary' title. This is an equitable title, which gives way to formal legal title in property.

Mabo is the surname of activist Eddie Mabo from Mer Island in the Torres Strait, who was the first Indigenous person to successfully claim Indigenous interest in land in the Australian courts. He spent his life as a trade unionist and land rights activist. Mabo died before the judgment was delivered by the High Court.

30. Irene Watson and Raw Law:

Irene Watson is one of the leading legal scholars in Australia. Watson is from the Tanganekald, Meintangk Boandik First Nations Peoples, of the Coorong and the south east of South Australia. She writes on Indigenous peoples in law in both the context of Australian law and international law.

In her seminal work, she explores the notion of *Raw Law*, an Indigenous ontology towards law as inseparable from other elements of life:

> 'Raw law is unlike the imposed colonial legal system. It is unclothed of rules and regulations. The law was created raw like the land and its peoples. Our law was birthed by creation. And like the birthing of people, the law was born naked. The law was at Kaldowinyeri naked, and is filled with the spirit of creation. The law is for the peoples to know and to live by as the ancestors had, from Kaldowinyeri. The raw law is not imposed, it is lived as a way of life.'
>
> Irene Watson, 'Kaldowinyeri – Munaintya: In the Beginning', (2000) 4 (1) *Flinders Journal of Law Reform*, 3, 3-4.

31. The Marital Rape Exemption

This refers to the act of sex with your spouse without consent. Historically, rape of one's spouse was either not a criminal offence, or marriage was considered a defence when an allegation of rape was made. This was based on social norms that a person (arguably a man) had a right to sex with his spouse. Across Australia this is now considered a form of both domestic violence and a criminal offence. However, criminalisation of this act only started occurring in Australian jurisdictions in 1981 and the High Court removed this defence in *Reg v L* (1991) 174 CLR 379.

32. Same Sex Marriage:

In 2017, the Australian government amended the legislative definition of marriage to be 'the union of two people to the exclusion of all others, voluntarily entered into for life'. This allowed people of the same sex to be legally recognised as married under the *Marriage Act 1961* (Cth). This amendment occurred after consistent and targeted lobbying by members of the LGBTQIA+ communities and their allies in Australia for a number of decades. As pressure mounted to recognise same sex marriage (as a number of overseas jurisdictions had done), the Australian government at first tried to insulate marriage in Australia from change. To shore up some ambiguities in the definition of marriage in the Constitution, in 2004 the Howard government introduced for the first time a legislative definition of marriage as being 'between a man and a woman' (section 5 *Marriage Act 1961* (Cth)). This definition reflected the traditional common law definition of marriage which had been applied since the decision of *Hyde v Hyde & Woodmansee* (1866) LR 1 P. & D. 130. This amendment prompted a number of constitutional challenges, including from States and Territories who wished to recognise same sex marriage. (*ACT v Commonwealth* [2013] HCA 55). Although these legal challenges failed, social pressure mounted to such an extent that the Australian government was forced to take action. It held a postal survey (which was called a plebiscite), asking the Australian public to indicate whether they would approve of same sex marriage. This mechanism was criticised for its departure from Australian voting processes, and also the exposure of same sex families to public opinion. The outcome of the plebiscite was positive, however, and the government honoured its commitment to change the definition of marriage.

33. The World Courts of Women:

The World Courts of Women are an alternative juridical forum that gives victims of violence who have been denied access to formal political and legal systems, or been traumatised by them, an opportunity for a public hearing.

They hold peoples' tribunals. For example, the 2015 session was held in Bangalore in India to witness gendered violence, and the 2012 court was held in California to witness poverty in the US. They don't carry the powers and sanctions of the state, but they are popular movements that bear witness to injustice.

Dr Corinne Kumar, who helped established the courts, describes it as:
'the unfolding of a space, an imaginary, a horizon, that invites us to think, to feel, to challenge, to connect. It is an attempt to define a new space for women, and to infuse this space with a new vision, a new politics. It is the gathering of

the voices and visions of the Global South, but locating itself in a discourse of dissent.' <https://www.youtube.com/watch?v-4uGSlaUTrJA>

34. Consent as a concept in sexual offences in law:

The criminal offence of sexual assault (or 'rape') has a long history. To be considered a criminal offence, there are usually two parts: an action (*actus reus*) and an accompanying intent to do the action (*mens rea*). In Australia, it has been characterised as an offence against a person, and its legal elements are generally described as acts of sexual intercourse without consent. In this way, consent has long been a key element in the determination of whether or not a criminal offence occurred. There are some categories of people who are deemed not to be able to consent, and these include young persons (typically under the age of 16).

Since the mental element of any crime focuses on the intent of the accused, then the question about whether or not a person consents to sexual intercourse is to be determined from the viewpoint of the accused. This has typically become phrased as whether the accused was aware that the person did not consent. Phrasing the question in this way has been problematic for victims of sexual assault, particularly as it focuses on what the victim did or didn't do or say to communicate to the accused that they did not consent. Informing the concept of consent are gendered myths about sex that have been challenged and exposed by many feminists such as: marriage means consent was always given, women lead men on into thinking they want sex by the way they dress or act, women are generally sexually available to men unless they clearly say no in ways that men comprehend in 'the heat of the moment', sex workers always consent to all men, women often make false allegations about rape later 'changing their minds' to ruin men's reputations. These myths meant that it was difficult for victims to prove that they did not consent. This contributed to victims experiencing trials as ordeals, and a very low rate of convictions.

The pressure created by feminists to better recognise the harm of sexual assault and women's experience of it, has led to a number of law reforms. Initially, these laws related to what assumptions can be drawn from evidence of the victim's behaviour, leading to directions being made to the jury to combat some of the common harmful gendered myths above. More recently, reforms have mostly focused on the definition of consent. For instance, some States and Territories in Australia have introduced a positive consent definition. This means that the accused can only rely on consent where it was positively communicated, rather than presumed from the circumstances. Further to that, the most recent reforms seek to define consent as something which must be both continuing and enthusiastically communicated, ensuring that the initiator of the sexual encounter takes responsibility in an ongoing way for consent.

See Nicola Lacey 'Unspeakable subjects, impossible rights: Sexuality, integrity and criminal law' (1998) 11 (1) *Canadian Journal of Law & Jurisprudence*, 47-48.

35 Legal and professional privilege:

Whilst the court has considerable powers to require individuals to present evidence relevant to a dispute (either orally or through documents), a request to produce evidence might be refused by a party on the grounds of 'privilege'. One ground of privilege is 'legal and professional privilege'. See for example, Part 3.10 *Evidence Act* (ACT). This privilege protects the disclosure of evidence to the court that was generated either through the provision of legal advice, or in preparation for litigation. The concern is that without the existence of 'legal and professional privilege', an individual would withhold facts from their lawyers and so would not obtain accurate legal advice. This in turn, might compromise the functioning of an adversarial legal system which relies on the effective pursuit of legal argument through debate often via legal representatives.

36. Chief Justice Kiefel

Chief Justice Kiefel left school at fifteen and then retrained as a lawyer while working as a secretary. Amongst other appointments, she served as a Judge on the Queensland Supreme Court and the Federal Court. With an outstanding legal career in a diverse range of positions, Kiefel was appointed to the High Court of Australia in 2007. In taking up the position, she was the third female Justice of the highest court in Australia. Later in 2017, she would become the first woman to be appointed as Chief Justice of that court. Commentators have noted that Kiefel's period as Chief Justice has been marked by a significant degree of collegiality in decision making.

In June 2020, Chief Justice Kiefel publicly announced that an inquiry had been held into the actions of a previous High Court Judge (Justice Heydon). The inquiry investigated whether whilst on the bench of the HCA, Justice Heydon had sexually harassed some court associates. Chief Justice Kiefel accepted and responded to the findings of that inquiry, issued a public apology and adopted the inquiry's recommendations.

37. Common Assault:

A common assault is a criminal offence that is considered less serious than an aggravated assault. To establish a common assault it must be proven beyond reasonable doubt that an assault occurred, and it was either intentionally violent or reckless.

Punching, kicking and spitting are often forms of common assault.

38. Boxventura de Sousa Santos

De Sousa Santos is a leading scholar in legal sociology and explores questions of epistemological violence and how this plays out in law. He explores the ways of thinking and being that shape dominant legal systems, and how that is harmful to people with other knowledge systems. He writes to issues that impact particularly on questions of law in the Global South. In *Epistemologies of the South* he states that:

see page 73

> 'All of our theoretical thinking in the global North has been based on the idea of an abyssal line. A line that is so important that it has remained invisible. It makes an invisible distinction sustaining all the distinctions we make between legal and illegal, and between scientific, theological and philosophical knowledges... All of our theories have been based and developed on the experiences from this side of the line. Our universalisms have been based on the realities of this side of the line; the other side of the line has remained invisible. This exclusion and silencing of the other side of the line is such that what happens there does not compromise the universality of our ideas, because they do not count as reality, because the people that live there do not count as humans in the modern understanding of humanity. The Western-centric conception of humanity is not possible without a concept of sub-humanity (a set of human groups that are not fully human, be they slaves, women, indigenous peoples, migrant workers, Muslims)' (p20-21)

39. Arturo Escobar:

Arturo Escobar is an American and Colombian scholar who writes on issues of epistemological and ontological violence and possibilities of transformation. In his book, *Designs for the Pluriverse*, he considers 'cultural, civilizational, and ecological transitions: an ontological approach to design and design for transitions: and the relations among autonomy, design, and the political activation of relational and communal logics at the center of the transitions.'

Arturo Escobar, *Designs for the Pluriverse: Radical Interdependence, Autonomy, and the Making of Worlds* (Duke University Press, 2018) xi.

<https://www.youtube.com/watch?v-8Ouy7aN6XPs>

40. Grace Tame:

Grace Tame is a well-known public figure in Australia. She is an activist and was instrumental in leading the campaign #letherspeak, where she successfully argued for reform of Tasmania's sexual assault laws which prevented sexual assault survivors naming convicted sexual assault offenders. She argued persuasively that this 'gag law' prevented sexual assault survivors from speaking out against them and the difficulties that they face, including challenges in seeking justice. Her passion and commitment to this campaign was informed by first hand experiences of sexual assault. The importance of her campaign was recognised, and she was awarded the accolade of 'Australian of the Year' in 2021. The following year, she was outspoken in her criticism of the Prime Minister's handling of allegations of sexual harassment in Parliament. While some criticised her for being party political, others lauded her courage to express her rage and anger at a time when women were being asked (again) to be patient and accept that change would be slow.

41. Pecuniary compensation:

Pecuniary generally refers to money. Pecuniary compensation refers to forms of compensation that relate to lost revenue and wages, for example.

42 Retribution as a sentencing principle:

Theories of retribution justify the punishment of an individual who does something wrong. Retribution is one of a number of theories of punishment in contemporary criminal law, which now include; rehabilitation, deterrence and incapacitation. These theories are present in the sentencing principles contained in Australian statutes. For example, Section 3A of the *Crimes (Sentencing Procedure) Act* 1999 (NSW) ('CSP Act') sets out the following seven purposes 'for which a court may impose an adequate punishment on an offender':

a) To ensure that the offender is adequately punished for the offence,
b) To prevent crime by deterring the offender and others from committing similar offences,
c) To protect the community from the offender,
d) To promote rehabilitation of the offender,
e) To make the offender accountable for his or her actions,
f) To denounce the offender's conduct, and
g) To recognise the harm done to the victim and the community.

Theories of retribution sit behind the NSW sentencing principles of a 'adequate punishment', 'holding the offender accountable', 'denouncing conduct' and 'recognising harm'. As articulated by the High Court in *Muldrock v The Queen* 'the purposes stated [in section 3A] are the familiar, overlapping and, at times, conflicting purposes of criminal punishment under the common law.' (*Muldrock v The Queen* (2012) 244 CLR 120 [20].)

See ALRC 'Family Violence: A National Legal Response' (2010, ALRC report 114 <https://www.alrc.gov.au/publication/family-violence-a-national-legal-response-alrc-report-114/4-purposes-of-laws-relevant-to-family-violence/criminal-law/#:~:text-4.82%20Retribution%E2%80%94often%20referred%20to,Leviticus%20in%20the%20Old%20Testament.>)

43. Robert Cover

Robert Cover was an American scholar who wrote about the relationship of law, interpretation and violence.

In his most renowned essay, *Violence and the Word*, he writes:

> 'Legal interpretation takes place in a field of pain and death. This is true in several senses. Legal interpretive acts signal and occasion the

imposition of violence upon others: A judge articulates her understanding of a text, and as a result, somebody loses his freedom, his property, his children, even his life. Interpretations in law also constitute justifications for violence which has already occurred or which is about to occur. When interpreters have finished their work, they frequently leave behind victims whose lives have been torn apart by these organized, social practices of violence. Neither legal interpretation nor the violence it occasions may be properly understood apart from one another.'

Robert Cover, 'Violence and the Word' (1986) 95 *Yale Law Journal*, 1601. <https://www.jstor.org/stable/796468>.

44 Standpoint theory:

Standpoint theory is a theory emerging from feminist and First Nations scholarship which argues that it is impossible to separate knowledge from subjective experience. Note that feminist standpoint theory and Indigenous standpoint theory have important differences. Rather than perform or suggest knowledge is objective, standpoint theory seeks to ground knowledge in the standpoint of the thinker. Moreton-Robinson says:

'An Indigenous women's standpoint is ascribed through inheritance and achieved through struggle. It is constituted by our sovereignty and constitutive of the interconnectedness of our ontology (our way of being); our epistemology (our way of knowing) and our axiology (our way of doing). It generates its problematics through Indigenous women's knowledges and experiences acknowledging that intersecting oppressions will situate us in different power relations and affect our different individual experiences under social, political, historical and material conditions that we share either consciously or unconsciously... Our lives are always shaped by the omnipresence of patriarchal white sovereignty and its continual denial of our sovereignty.'

Aileen Moreton-Robinson, 'Towards an Australian Indigenous Women's Standpoint Theory', (2013) 28 (73) *Australian Feminist Studies*, 331, 340. <http://doi.org/br2h>.

(Sarouche's Maja Milatovic quote comes from 'The Love of Women, Kind as Well as Cruel: Feminist Alliances and Contested Spaces in Audre Lorde's "Zami: A New Spelling of My Name"', *Eurozine*, (2015) 3 <https://www.eurozine.com/the-love-of-women-kind-as-well-as-cruel/?pdf>.)

45. Sisters Inside
END TOXIC PRISONS
BLOW UP &
THE PIPELINE

Sisters Inside was established in 1992 as a community organisation to support criminalised women and girls in Queensland. Within the platform of its mission are social justice values such as fighting racism, injustice and poverty. Sisters Inside holds regular conferences that receive international attention on issues of abolition, prison, gender violence and justice.

46. The sexual
assault allegations
against former
Justice Heydon.

In June 2020, Chief Justice Kiefel (see entry #36 above) publicly announced that an independent inquiry had investigated the actions of a previous High Court Judge (Justice Heydon). The inquiry had found that he had sexually harassed six High Court Associates. Chief Justice Kiefel stated that she accepted the recommendations of the inquiry and issued a public apology. In her announcement, she stated that 'We know it would have been difficult to come forward. Their accounts of their experiences at the time have been believed.' Justice Heydon denied that he had sexually harassed any court associates.

<https://www.abc.net.au/news/2020-06-22/former-high-court-judge-sexually-harrassed-several-associates/12381236>

In memory of Zöe "Sparrow" Hulme-Peake

Blockade Australia climate activist, pirate and friend.

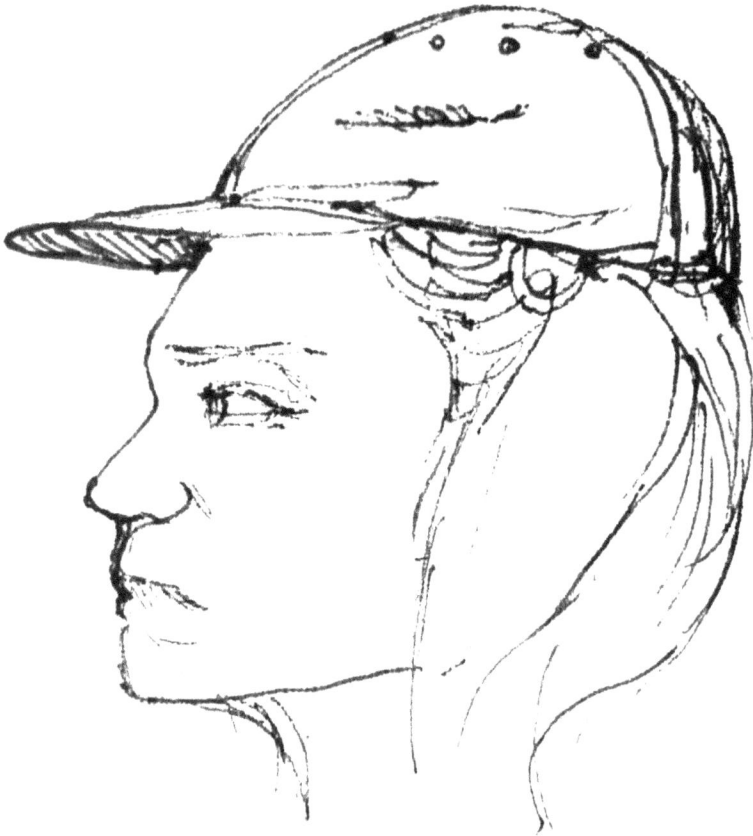

20 July 2001 — 4 September 2023